The Little Book of Success Quotes

The Little Book of Success Quotes is available at special discounts
when purchased in quantities for educational use, fund-raising or
sales promotions. Special editions or book excerpts can also be
created. For more information, please contact
inspire@littlequotebooks.com.

ISBN-10: 0615516815
EAN-13: 9780615516813

Library of Congress Control Number: 2011934906
Little Quote Books, Chicago, IL

www.littlequotebooks.com

The
Little Book
of
Success
Quotes

Edited by Kathleen Welton

Table of Contents

Thank You vii

Introduction ix

❀ Aim High. 1

❀ Follow Your Heart. 9

❀ Healthy, Wealthy, and Wise 17

❀ The Journey 25

❀ Knowledge. 33

❀ Life: It Goes On. 41

❀ Little by Little 49

❀ Live. Love. Laugh 57

❀ Overcoming Obstacles 65

❀ The Secret of Success. 73

❀ Simplicity. 81

❀ Win or Lose 89

Appendix: Favorite Quotes. 99

Appendix: Success Checklist 101

Appendix: Success Journal 107

Biographical Index 113

Index 123

Thank You

With appreciation to the authors and teachers that came before us to record their simple, classic, and inspirational thoughts. *Thanks for everything* to my family and friends.

Introduction

This is a collection of 365 quotes—a quote to use as inspiration to enjoy each day of every month of the year. Quotes have been selected to cover a dozen topics. They are arranged for easy access as follows:

* ❀ Aim High
* ❀ Follow Your Heart
* ❀ Healthy, Wealthy, and Wise
* ❀ The Journey
* ❀ Knowledge
* ❀ Life: It Goes On
* ❀ Little by Little
* ❀ Live. Love. Laugh.
* ❀ Overcoming Obstacles
* ❀ The Secret of Success
* ❀ Simplicity
* ❀ Win or Lose

The quotes are arranged alphabetically by author in each section, so that you can easily find your favorites by author and by topic.

While there is no single recipe for success—I do believe that it is possible to create an individual definition of what success is—and to apply this definition to all areas of your life. As such, this book shares ideas of what success can be as it relates to business, careers, health, leadership, life, relationships, sports, wealth, and more.

In addition to 365 favorite quotes, the book includes a section to record favorite quotes, a monthly success journal, as well as a success checklist to keep track of your progress in life including events, little things, and situations that have been especially important.

The authors and quotes that appear in this little book have been selected for a variety of reasons. Some represent lessons learned over the years from "the school of hard knocks." Some continue to serve as my life-long favorites (in addition to those included in *The Little Book of Gratitude Quotes*). And others have been selected to serve as inspiration for success in the years ahead. Collecting quotes—like success—is a work in progress. Here's to your continued success!

Enjoy the journey,
Kathleen Welton

Aim High

Hope is the dream of the waking man.

~Aristotle

Any great work of art...revives and readapts time and space, and the measure of its success is the extent to which it makes you an inhabitant of that world—the extent to which it invites you in and lets you breathe its strange, special air.

~Leonard Bernstein

Make no little plans; they have no magic to stir men's blood and probably themselves will not be realized. Make big plans; aim high in hope and work, remembering that a noble, logical diagram once recorded will not die, but long after we are gone be a living thing, asserting itself with ever-growing insistence.

~David Burnham

Aim for the highest.
~Andrew Carnegie

༄

Dream as if you'll live forever, live as if you'll die today.
~James Dean

༄

Courage is the price that life exacts for granting peace.
~Amelia Earhart

༄

Try not to become a man of success,
but rather try to become a man of value.
~Albert Einstein

༄

Every artist was first an amateur.
~Ralph Waldo Emerson

Hitch your wagon to a star.
~Ralph Waldo Emerson

༄

The whole secret of a successful life is to find out what it is
one's destiny to do, and then do it.
~Henry Ford

༄

Success in its highest and noblest form calls for peace of mind and enjoyment and happiness which come only to the man who has found the work that he likes best.

~*Napoleon Hill*

∽

Every calling is great when greatly pursued.

~*Oliver Wendell Holmes, Sr.*

∽

The sculptor produces the beautiful statue by chipping away such parts of the marble block as are not needed—it is a process of elimination.

~*Elbert Hubbard*

∽

Do not let it be your aim to be something, but to be someone.

~*Victor Hugo*

∽

We're here to make a dent in the universe. Otherwise why even be here?

~*Steve Jobs*

∽

Let every nation know, whether it wishes us well or ill, we shall pay any price, bear any burden, meet any hardship, support any friend, oppose any foe, in order to assure the survival and the success of liberty.

~John Fitzgerald Kennedy

∽

Ideas shape the course of history.

~John Maynard Keynes

∽

The art of acceptance is the art of making someone who has just done you a small favor wish that he might have done you a greater one.

~Martin Luther King, Jr.

∽

Always bear in mind that your own resolution to succeed is more important than any one thing.

~Abraham Lincoln

∽

Happiness can exist only in acceptance.

~George Orwell

∽

Believe in yourself! Have faith in your abilities! Without a humble but reasonable confidence in your own powers you cannot be successful or happy.

~*Norman Vincent Peale*

∞

The artist is a receptacle for the emotions that come from all over the place: from the sky, from the earth, from a scrap of paper, from a passing shape, from a spider's web.

~*Pablo Picasso*

∞

Beauty lies in Simplicity.

~*Proverb*

∞

Aim for the moon. If you miss, you may hit a star.

~*W. Clement Stone*

∞

The greater man the greater courtesy.

~*Alfred Lord Tennyson*

∞

Dreams are the touchstones of our character.

~*Henry David Thoreau*

∞

Be content with what you have, rejoice in the way things are. When you realize there is nothing lacking, the whole world belongs to you.

~Lao Tzu

Some people dream of success...while others wake up and work hard at it.

~Author Unknown

They can because they think they can.

~Virgil

The grateful mind is constantly fixed upon the best. Therefore it tends to become the best. It takes the form or character of the best, and will receive the best.

~Wallace D. Wattles

In dreams begins responsibility.

~William Butler Yeats

Follow Your Heart

Independence is happiness.

~Susan B. Anthony

Whatever a person frequently thinks and reflects on, that will
become the inclination of their mind.

~Buddha

Does this path have a heart? If it does, the path
is good; if it doesn't, it is of no use.

~Carlos Castaneda

To put the world right in order, we must first put the nation in
order; to put the nation in order, we must first put the family
in order; to put the family in order, we must first cultivate our
personal life; we must first set our hearts right.

~Confucius

By not caring too much about what people think, I'm able to think for myself and propagate ideas which are very often unpopular. And I succeed.

~Albert Ellis

∽

Nothing astonishes men so much as common sense and plain dealing.

~Ralph Waldo Emerson

∽

My aim is to put down on paper what I see and what I feel in the best and simplest way.

~Ernest Hemingway

∽

No man has a chance to enjoy permanent success until he begins to look in the mirror for the real cause of all his mistakes.

~Napoleon Hill

Service, Sacrifice and Self-Control are three words which must be well understood by the person who succeeds in doing something that is of help to this world.

~Napoleon Hill

∽

Have the courage to act instead of react.

~*Oliver Wendell Holmes, Sr.*

∽

Your time is limited, so don't waste it living someone else's life. Don't be trapped by dogma—which is living with the results of other people's thinking. Don't let the noise of other's opinions drown out your own inner voice. And most important, have the courage to follow your heart and intuition. They somehow already know what you truly want to become. Everything else is secondary.

~*Steve Jobs*

∽

Ambition is so powerful a passion in the human breast, that however high we reach we are never satisfied.

~*Henry Wadsworth Longfellow*

∽

The great lesson...is that the sacred is in the ordinary, that it is to be found in one's daily life, in one's neighbors, friends, and family, in one's back yard.

~*Abraham Maslow*

∽

Gratitude is the memory of the heart.

~*Jean Massieu*

∽

There is only one success—to be able to
spend your life in your own way.

~*Christopher Morley*

∽

The more intensely we feel about an idea or a goal, the more as-
suredly the idea, buried deep in our subconscious, will direct us
along the path to its fulfillment.

~*Earl Nightingale*

∽

Empty pockets never held anyone back. Only empty heads
and empty hearts can do that.

~*Norman Vincent Peale*

∽

Be not the first by whom the new are tried,
Nor yet the last to lay the old aside.

~*Alexander Pope*

∽

Do what you feel in your heart to be right—for you'll be criti-
cized anyway. You'll be damned if you do,
and damned if you don't.

~*Eleanor Roosevelt*

∽

And you? When will you begin
that long journey into yourself?
~Rumi

∽

You have brains in your head. You have feet in your shoes. You
can steer yourself any direction you choose. You're on your own,
and you know what you know. And you are the guy who'll
decide where to go.

~Dr. Seuss

∽

Our doubts are traitors, and make us lose the good we oft
might win, by fearing to attempt.

~William Shakespeare

∽

The best things in life are nearest: Breath in your nostrils, light
in your eyes, flowers at your feet, duties at your hand, the path
of right just before you. Then do not grasp at the stars, but do
life's plain, common work as it comes, certain that daily duties
and daily bread are the sweetest things in life.

~Robert Louis Stevenson

∽

Judge your success by what you had to give up in
order to get it.

~Author Unknown

You can close your eyes to things you don't want to see, but you can't close your heart to the things you don't want to feel.

~Author Unknown

∞

Simplicity is the ultimate sophistication.

~Leonardo da Vinci

∞

Whatever satisfies the soul is truth.

~Walt Whitman

∞

Life is not complex. We are complex. Life is simple, and the simple thing is the right thing.

~Oscar Wilde

Healthy, Wealthy, and Wise

A faithful friend is the medicine of life.

~Bible, Ecclesiasticus 6:16

The secret of health for both mind and body is not to mourn for the past, not to worry about the future, or not to anticipate troubles, but to live in the present moment wisely and earnestly.

~Buddha

Never continue in a job you don't enjoy. If you're happy in what you're doing, you'll like yourself, you'll have inner peace. And if you have that, along with physical health, you will have had more success than you could possibly have imagined.

~Johnny Carson

Business, that's easily defined—it's other people's money.

~Peter Drucker

Beware of little expenses. A small leak will
sink a great ship.

~Benjamin Franklin

Early to bed and early to rise, makes a man
healthy, wealthy, and wise.

~Benjamin Franklin

In this world, nothing is certain but death and taxes.

~Benjamin Franklin

A penny saved is a penny earned.

~Benjamin Franklin

❦

If money is your hope for independence you will never have it.
The only real security that a man will have in this world is a
reserve of knowledge, experience, and ability.

~Henry Ford

❦

There needs to be bolder thinking,...on how to measure the
quality of life of men and women in the work force. Currently,
success is measured by material advancements. We need to
readjust the definition of success to account for time outside of
work and satisfaction of life, not just the
dollars-and-cents bottom line.

~Betty Friedan

❦

No one can possibly achieve any real and lasting
success or "get rich" in business by being a conformist.

~J. Paul Getty

∽

You can't connect the dots looking forward; you can only connect them looking backwards. So you have to trust that the
dots will somehow connect in your future. You have to trust in
something—your gut, destiny, life, karma, whatever. This ap-
proach has never let me down, and it has
made all the difference in my life.

~Steve Jobs

∽

The more things change, the more they remain the same.

~Alphonse Karr

∽

If you work just for money, you'll never make it, but if you love
what you're doing and you always put the customer
first, success will be yours.

~Ray Kroc

∽

It is easier to be wise on behalf of others than
for ourselves.

~François Duc de la Rochefoucauld

∽

Give what you have to somebody,
it may be better than you think.

~*Henry Wadsworth Longfellow*

൞

He, who has health, has hope; and he
who has hope has everything.

~*Arabian Proverb*

Don't put all your eggs in one basket.

~*Proverb*

൞

Giving is the secret of a healthy life. Not necessarily money, but
whatever a man has of encouragement and
sympathy and understanding.

~*John D. Rockefeller, Jr.*

൞

Don't gamble; take all your savings and buy some
good stock and hold it till it goes up, then sell it.
If it don't go up, don't buy it.

~*Will Rogers*

൞

There is no wealth but life.

~*John Ruskin*

൞

It is not the man who has too little, but
the man who desires more, that is poor.

~Seneca

∽

True wisdom comes to each of us when we realize
how little we understand about life, ourselves, and
the world around us.

~Socrates

∽

Who is rich? He that rejoices in his portion.

~The Talmud

∽

October. This is one of the peculiarly dangerous months to
speculate in stocks in. The others are July, January, September,
April, November, May, March, June, December,
August, and February.

~Mark Twain

∽

He who obtains has little. He who scatters has much.

~Lao Tzu

∽

It is wise to keep in mind that no
success or failure is necessarily final.

~Author Unknown

The excellence of a gift lies in its
appropriateness rather than in its value.

~Charles Dudley Warner

Behold I do not give lectures or a little charity,
When I give I give myself.

~Walt Whitman

I adore simple pleasures. They are the last healthy refuge
in a complex world.

~Oscar Wilde

The world is too much with us; late and soon,
Getting and spending, we lay waste our powers:
Little we see in Nature that is ours.

~William Wordsworth

The Journey

Success is a journey, not a destination.
The doing is often more important than the outcome.

~Arthur Ashe

Every day is a journey, and the journey itself is home.

~Matsuo Bashō

Measure not the work
until the day's out and the labor done.

~Elizabeth Barrett Browning

It is better to travel well than to arrive.

~Buddha

"Would you tell me, please, which way I ought to go from here?"
"That depends a good deal on where you want to
get to," said the (Cheshire) Cat.
"I don't much care where—" said Alice.
"Then it doesn't much matter which
way you go," said the Cat.

~*Lewis Carroll*

∽

Success is not final, failure is not fatal: it
is the courage to continue that counts.

~*Winston S. Churchill*

∽

The ideals which have lighted my way, and time after time have
given me new courage to face life cheerfully, have been Kindness, Beauty, and Truth. The trite subjects of human efforts,
possessions, outward success, luxury have always
seemed to me contemptible.

~*Albert Einstein*

∽

The measure of a great leader, is
their success in bringing everyone
around to their opinion twenty years later.

~*Ralph Waldo Emerson*

∽

There are no gains without pains.

~Benjamin Franklin

∽

It's not where we stand but in what direction we are moving.

~Johann Wolfgang von Goethe

∽

Peace is a journey of a thousand miles and it must be taken one step at a time.

~Lyndon B. Johnson

∽

I am a great believer in luck, and I find the harder I work the more I have of it.

~Stephen Leacock

∽

Success is going from failure to failure without losing your enthusiasm.

~Abraham Lincoln

∽

Each failure to sell will increase your chances for success at your next attempt.

~Og Mandino

The victory of success is half won when one gains the habit of setting goals and achieving them. Even the most tedious chore will become endurable as you parade through each day convinced that every task, no matter how menial or boring, brings you closer to fulfilling your dreams.

~Og Mandino

ﾍﾉ

The only joy in the world is to begin.

~Cesare Pavese

ﾍﾉ

Life is just a journey.

~Princess Diana

ﾍﾉ

When you have completed 95 percent of your journey, you are only halfway there.

~Japanese Proverb

You can lead a horse to water, but you can't make it drink.

~Proverb

Failure is the stepping stone for success.

~Proverb

Never put off till tomorrow what you can do today.

~Proverb

ﾍﾉ

The ladder of success is best climbed by
stepping on the rungs of opportunity.

~Ayn Rand

∽

A little simplification would be the first
step toward rational living, I think.

~Eleanor Roosevelt

∽

Does the road wind up-hill all the way?
Yes, to the very end.
Will the day's journey take the whole long day?
From morn to night, my friend.

~Christina Rossetti

∽

I'm an idealist. I don't know where I'm
going, but I'm on my way.

~Carl Sandburg

∽

Beware the barrenness of a busy life.

~Socrates

∽

Don't judge each day by the harvest you reap but by the seeds
that you plant.

~*Robert Louis Stevenson*

∽

Everyone thinks of changing the world, but no one thinks of
changing himself.

~*Leo Tolstoy*

∽

If nothing ever changed, there'd be no butterflies.

~*Author Unknown*

∽

Simplicity is making the journey of this life with just baggage
enough.

~*Charles Dudley Warner*

Knowledge

Knowledge is power.

~*Francis Bacon*

When you know a thing, to hold that you know it; and when you do not know a thing, to allow that you do not know it—this is knowledge.

~*Confucius*

To successfully respond to the myriad of changes that shake the world, transformation into a new style of management is required. The route to take is what I call profound knowledge—knowledge for leadership of transformation.

~*W. Edwards Deming*

It is not enough to have a good mind.
The main thing is to use it well.

~René Descartes

∽

We never know, believe me, when we have
succeeded best.

~Miguel de Unamuno

∽

Nature is what we know—
Yet have no art to say—
So impotent Our Wisdom is
To her Simplicity.

~Emily Dickinson

∽

As a general rule, the most successful man
in life is the man who has the best information.

~Benjamin Disraeli

∽

If A is success in life, then A equals x plus y plus z.
Work is x; y is play; and z is keeping your mouth shut.

~Albert Einstein

The only source of knowledge is experience.

~Albert Einstein

There is only one road to human greatness: through
the school of hard knocks.

~Albert Einstein

♋

Teach us to care and not to care
Teach us to sit still.

~T.S. Eliot

♋

An investment in knowledge always pays the best interest.

~Benjamin Franklin

♋

For beautiful eyes, look for the good in others; for beautiful
lips, speak only words of kindness; and for poise, walk with the
knowledge that you are never alone.

~Audrey Hepburn

♋

It is the province of knowledge to speak,
and it is the privilege of wisdom to listen.

~Oliver Wendell Holmes, Sr.

♋

Leadership and learning are indispensable to each other.

~John Fitzgerald Kennedy

♋

I do the very best I know how—the very best I can;
and I mean to keep on doing so until the end.

~Abraham Lincoln

You can fool all the people some of the time, and
some of the people all the time, but you cannot fool
all the people all the time.

~Abraham Lincoln

ᔡ

The difference between a successful person and others is not a
lack of strength, not a lack of knowledge, but
rather a lack of will.

~Vince Lombardi

ᔡ

Success is that old ABC—ability, breaks, and courage.

~Charles Luckman

ᔡ

Never doubt that a small group of thoughtful,
committed citizens can change the world.
Indeed, it is the only thing that ever has.

~Margaret Mead

ᔡ

80 percent of output is produced by 20 percent of input.

~ Vilfredo Pareto

ᔡ

Carry out a random act of kindness, with no expectation of reward, safe in the knowledge that one day someone might do the same for you.

~Princess Diana

༄

Actions speak louder than words.

~Proverb

Nothing succeeds like success.

~Proverb

༄

A man can learn only two ways, one by reading, and the other by association with smarter people.

~Will Rogers

༄

Remember always that you not only have the right to be an individual, you have an obligation to be one.

~Eleanor Roosevelt

༄

I was gratified to be able to answer promptly, and I did. I said I didn't know.

~Mark Twain

༄

The farther you go, the less you know.

~Lao Tzu

Even the knowledge of my own fallibility cannot keep me from making mistakes. Only when I fall do I get up again.

~Vincent van Gogh

Let sleeping dogs lie.

~Robert Walpole

What is a cynic? A man who knows the price of everything, and the value of nothing.

~Oscar Wilde

Life: It Goes On

Very little is needed to make a happy life; it is all
within yourself, in your way of thinking.

~Marcus Aurelius

The art of living is more like wrestling than dancing.

~Marcus Aurelius

Life consists not in holding good cards but
in playing those you hold well.

~Josh Billings

Life is a tragedy when seen in close-up,
but a comedy in long-shot.

~Charlie Chaplin

A vocabulary of truth and simplicity will
be of service throughout your life.

~Winston Churchill

ᔕ

Life is really simple, but we insist on making it complicated.

~Confucius

ᔕ

A man who dares to waste one hour of time has not discovered
the value of life.

~Charles Darwin

ᔕ

The best years of your life are the ones in which you
decide your problems are your own. You don't blame
them on your mother, the ecology,
or the president. You realize that you
control your own destiny.

~Albert Ellis

ᔕ

All life is an experiment. The more
experiments you make the better.

~Ralph Waldo Emerson

ᔕ

The main facts in human life are five:
birth, food, sleep, love and death.

~*E. M. Forster*

∽

In three words I can sum up everything
I've learned about life: it goes on.

~**Robert Frost**

∽

My formula for living is quite simple. I get up
in the morning and I go to bed at night.
In between, I occupy myself as best I can.

~**Cary Grant**

∽

Life is half spent before we know what it is.

~**George Herbert**

∽

The great use of life is to spend it for
something that will outlast it.

~**William James**

∽

The shoe that fits one person pinches another;
there is no recipe for living that suits all cases.

~Carl Jung

∾

Science is organized knowledge. Wisdom is organized life.

~Immanuel Kant

∾

Life is a succession of lessons which
must be lived to be understood.

~Helen Keller

∾

Life can only be understood backwards;
but it must be lived forwards.

~Søren Kierkegaard

∾

Life is real! Life is earnest!
And the grave is not its goal;
Dust thou art, to dust returnest,
Was not spoken of the soul.

~Henry Wadsworth Longfellow

∾

Nothing is unthinkable, nothing impossible to the balanced person, provided it arises out of the needs of life and is dedicated to life's further developments.

~Lewis Mumford

∾

Life must be lived as play.

~Plato

∾

Time is the coin of your life. It is the only coin you have, and only you can determine how it will be spent.

~Carl Sandburg

∾

We are such stuff
As dreams are made on, and our little life
Is rounded with a sleep.

~William Shakespeare

∾

There is only one difference between a long life and a good dinner: that, in the dinner, the sweets come last.

~Robert Louis Stevenson

∾

May you live all the days of your life.

~Jonathan Swift

Life is but thought.

~Sara Teasdale

As you simplify your life, the laws of the universe
will be simpler; solitude will not be solitude, poverty
will not be poverty, nor weakness weakness.

~Henry David Thoreau

The price of anything is the amount of
life you exchange for it.

~Henry David Thoreau

The two hardest things to handle in life are failure and success.

~Author Unknown

If your mind isn't clouded by unnecessary things, this is the
best season of your life.

~Wu Men

Little by Little

Ability is of little account without opportunity.

~Lucille Ball

The greatest things ever done on Earth have
been done little by little.

~William Jennings Bryan

I still get wildly enthusiastic about little things... I
play with leaves. I skip down the street and run
against the wind.

~Leo Buscaglia

There is little success where there is little laughter.

~Andrew Carnegie

Do your duty and a little more and
the future will take care of itself.

~Andrew Carnegie

❧

Speak the truth, do not yield to anger; give, if thou
art asked for little; by these three steps thou wilt
go near the gods.

~Confucius

❧

To live is so startling it leaves little
time for anything else.

~Emily Dickinson

❧

Genius at first is little more than a great capacity for receiving
discipline.

~George Eliot

❧

The essence of philosophy is that a man
should so live that his happiness shall depend as
little as possible on external things.

~Epictetus

❧

The man who will use his skill and constructive imagination to see how much he can give for a dollar, instead of how little he can give for a dollar, is bound to succeed.

~Henry Ford

There are no big problems, there are just a lot of little problems.

~Henry Ford

∽

Little said is soon amended. There is always time to add a word, never to withdraw one.

~Baltasar Gracián

∽

Imagination is the key to my lyrics. The rest is painted with a little science fiction.

~Jimi Hendrix

∽

Big pay and little responsibility are circumstances seldom found together.

~Napoleon Hill

∽

A little more persistence, a little more effort, and what seemed hopeless failure may turn to glorious success.

~Elbert Hubbard

∽

You've got to work things out in the cloakroom, and when
you've got them worked out, you can debate a
little before you vote.

~Lyndon B. Johnson

∽

Do not accustom yourself to use big words for little matters.

~Samuel Johnson

∽

There are many little ways to enlarge your child's world. Love of
books is the best of all.

~Jackie Kennedy

∽

The biggest human temptation is to settle for too little.

~Thomas Merton

∽

No one ever told me I was pretty when I was a little girl. All
little girls should be told they're pretty, even if they aren't.

~Marilyn Monroe

∽

Just because I managed to do a little something, I don't want
anyone back home to think I got the big head.

~Elvis Presley

∽

If a little dreaming is dangerous, the cure for it is not
to dream less but to dream more, to dream
all the time.

~Marcel Proust

Time passes, and little by little everything that
we have spoken in falsehood becomes true.

~Marcel Proust

❧

Great oaks from little acorns grow.

~Proverb

❧

Sometimes I wonder if we shall ever grow up in our politics and
say definite things which mean something, or whether we shall
always go on using generalities to which everyone can subscribe,
and which mean very little.

~Eleanor Roosevelt

❧

Each day is a little life: every waking and rising a little birth,
every fresh morning a little youth, every going to rest and sleep
a little death.

~Arthur Schopenhauer

❧

Men do change, and change comes like a little wind that ruffles the curtains at dawn, and it comes like the stealthy perfume of wildflowers hidden in the grass.

~John Steinbeck

Big doors swing on little hinges.

~W. Clement Stone

So many worlds, so much to do,
So little done, such things to be.
~Alfred Lord Tennyson

You can always amend a big plan, but you can never expand a little one. I don't believe in little plans. I believe in plans big enough to meet a situation which we can't possibly foresee now.

~Harry S. Truman

Labor to keep alive in your breast that little spark of celestial fire, called conscience.

~George Washington

Live. Love. Laugh.

Life is short and we have never too much time for gladdening
the hearts of those who are traveling the dark journey with us.
Oh, be swift to love, make haste to be kind.

~Henri-Frédéric Amiel

Imagination was given to man to
compensate him for what he is not; a sense of
humor to console him for what he is.

~Francis Bacon

But the fruit of the Spirit is love, joy, peace,
patience, kindness, goodness, faithfulness,
gentleness, self-control.

~Bible, Galatians 5

Love is patient, love is kind. It does not envy,
it does not boast …It always protects, always trusts,
always hopes, always perseveres.

~Bible, 1 Corinthians 13

Blessed are you who weep now, for you shall laugh.

~*Bible, Luke 6*

∽

When you have once seen the glow of happiness on the face of a beloved person, you know that a man can have no vocation but to awaken that light on the faces surrounding him.

~*Albert Camus*

∽

How far you go in life depends on your being tender with the young, compassionate with the aged, sympathetic with the striving, and tolerant of the weak and strong. Because someday in your life you will have been all of these.

~*George Washington Carver*

∽

I feel the capacity to care is the thing which gives life its deepest significance.

~*Pablo Casals*

∽

Life is just a bowl of cherries, don't take it serious, it's mysterious. Life is just a bowl of cherries, so live and laugh and laugh at love, love a laugh, laugh and love.

~*Bob Fosse*

∽

Wisdom ceases to be wisdom when it becomes too proud to weep, too grave to laugh, and too selfish to seek other than itself.

~Kahlil Gibran

Let there be spaces in your togetherness.

~Kahlil Gibran

❧

I love people who make me laugh. I honestly think it's the thing I like most, to laugh. It cures a multitude of ills. It's probably the most important thing in a person.

~Audrey Hepburn

❧

I have seen what a laugh can do. It can transform almost unbearable tears into something bearable, even hopeful.

~Bob Hope

❧

With the fearful strain that is on me night and day, if I did not laugh I should die.

~Abraham Lincoln

❧

The older you get the stronger the wind gets—and it's always in your face.

~Pablo Picasso

❧

Many a true word is spoken in jest.

~Proverb

༉

There's a thin line between to laugh with and to laugh at.

~Richard Pryor

༉

The giving of love is an education in itself.

~Eleanor Roosevelt

༉

Love all, trust a few, do wrong to none.

~William Shakespeare

Brevity is the soul of wit.

~William Shakespeare

Simply the thing that I am shall make me live.

~William Shakespeare

༉

Trouble is part of your life—if you don't share it, you don't give the person who loves you a chance to love you enough.

~Dinah Shore

༉

The problem with people who have no vices is that generally you can be pretty sure they're going to have some pretty annoying virtues.

~Elizabeth Taylor

༄

It's not how much you do, but how much love you put into what you do that counts.

~Mother Teresa

༄

Oh, somewhere in this favored land the sun is shining bright;
The band is playing somewhere, and somewhere hearts are light,
And somewhere men are laughing, and little children shout;
But there is no joy in Mudville—mighty Casey has struck out.

~Ernest L. Thayer

༄

Humor is the great thing, the saving thing. The minute it crops up, all our irritation and resentments slip away, and a sunny spirit takes their place.

~Mark Twain

༄

You've got to take the good with the bad, smile with the sad, love what you've got, and remember what you had. Always forgive, but never forget. Learn from mistakes, but never regret.

~Author Unknown

Every survival kit should include a sense of humor.

~Author Unknown

Live and let live.

~Author Unknown

To make mistakes is human; to stumble is commonplace; to be able to laugh at yourself is maturity.

~William Arthur Ward

Be obscure clearly.

~E. B. White

Overcoming Obstacles

A high heart ought to bear calamities and not flee them, since in bearing them appears the grandeur of the mind and in fleeing them the cowardice of the heart.

~Pietro Aretino

A wise man will make more opportunities than he finds.

~Francis Bacon

There are two ways of meeting difficulties: You alter the difficulties or you alter yourself to meet them.

~Phyllis Bottome

Act as if it were impossible to fail.

~Dorothea Brande

Do not dwell in the past, do not dream of the future, concentrate the mind on the present moment.

~Buddha

∽

The pessimist sees difficulty in every opportunity.
The optimist sees the opportunity in every difficulty.

~Winston Churchill

The farther backward you can look,
the farther forward you can see.

~Winston Churchill

∽

Three Rules of Work: Out of clutter find simplicity; From discord find harmony; In the middle of difficulty lies opportunity.

~Albert Einstein

Great spirits have always encountered
violent opposition from mediocre minds.

~Albert Einstein

In the middle of difficulty lies opportunity.

~Albert Einstein

∽

It is difficulties that show what men are.

~Epictetus

∽

First they ignore you, then they laugh at you,
then they fight you, then you win.

~Mahatma Gandhi

They cannot take away our self-respect
if we do not give it to them.

~Mahatma Gandhi

∽

If you don't stand for something, you will fall for anything.

~Alexander Hamilton

∽

Rise above principle and do what's right.

~Joseph Heller

∽

Nothing is impossible, the word itself says "I'm possible!"

~Audrey Hepburn

As you grow older, you will discover that you have two hands,
one for helping yourself, the other for helping others.

~Audrey Hepburn

∽

Is it not strange that we fear most that which never happens?
That we destroy our initiative by the fear of defeat, when, in
reality, defeat is a most useful tonic and should
be accepted as such.

~Napoleon Hill

Don't be afraid of a little opposition. Remember that the "Kite"
of Success generally rises against the wind
of Adversity—not with it!

~Napoleon Hill

✎

Little minds are tamed and subdued by misfortune;
but great minds rise above them.

~Washington Irving

✎

You will succeed if you persevere; and you will
find joy in overcoming obstacles.

~Helen Keller

✎

Let us never negotiate out of fear.
But let us never fear to negotiate.

~John Fitzgerald Kennedy

✎

Entrepreneurs are simply those who understand that there is little difference between obstacle and opportunity and are able to turn both to their advantage.

~Niccolò Machiavelli

ॐ

I have learned over the years that when one's mind is made up, this diminishes fear; knowing what must be done does away with fear.

~Rosa Parks

ॐ

The darkest hour is just before the dawn.

~Proverb

If you want to be respected, you must respect yourself.

~Spanish Proverb

ॐ

Fortune favors the brave.

~Terence

ॐ

Where there's a will, there's a way.

~Author Unknown

ॐ

Patience serves as a protection against wrongs as clothes do against cold. For it you put on more clothes as the cold increases, it will have no power to hurt you. So in like manner you must grow in patience when you meet with great wrongs, and they will then be powerless to vex your mind.

~*Leonardo da Vinci*

Success is to be measured not so much by the position that one has reached in life as by the obstacles which he has overcome while trying to succeed.

~*Booker T. Washington*

The Secret of Success

The ability to convert ideas to things
is the secret of outward success.
~Henry Ward Beecher

The toughest thing about success is that
you've got to keep on being a success.
~Irving Berlin

The secret of joy in work is contained in
one word—excellence. To know how to do
something well is to enjoy it.
~Pearl S. Buck

Flaming enthusiasm, backed up by horse sense and persistence,
is the quality that most frequently makes for success.
~Dale Carnegie

Success is getting what you want;
happiness is wanting what you get.

~*Dale Carnegie*

∾

Success consists of going from failure to
failure without loss of enthusiasm.

~*Winston Churchill*

∾

Success is more permanent when you achieve
it without destroying your principles.

~*Walter Cronkite*

∾

Fame is a bee.
It has a song—
It has a sting—
Ah, too, it has a wing.

~*Emily Dickinson*

∾

Everything should be made as simple as
possible, but not simpler.

~*Albert Einstein*

∾

Success seems to be largely a matter of
hanging on after others have let go.

~*William Feather*

∾

What is success? It is a toy
balloon among children armed with pins.

~*Gene Fowler*

∾

Everything is both simpler than we can imagine, and more
complicated that we can conceive.

~*Johann Wolfgang von Goethe*

∾

Pray that success will not come any faster
than you are able to endure it.

~*Elbert Hubbard*

∾

Innovation distinguishes between a leader and a follower.

~*Steve Jobs*

∾

Character cannot be developed in ease and quiet.
Only through experience of trial and suffering
can the soul be strengthened, vision cleared,
ambition inspired, and success achieved.

~Helen Keller

૭∾૭

Teach us Delight in the simple things,
And Mirth that has no bitter springs;
Forgiveness free of evil done,
And Love to all men 'neath the sun!

~Rudyard Kipling

૭∾૭

The two most important requirements for major success are:
first, being in the right place at the right time, and
second, doing something about it.

~Ray Kroc

૭∾૭

Always bear in mind that your own resolution to succeed is
more important than any other one thing.

~Abraham Lincoln

૭∾૭

Success is how high you bounce when you hit bottom.

~George Smith Patton

૭∾૭

To follow, without halt, one aim: There's the secret of success.

~Anna Pavlova

∽

The secret of success of consistency of purpose.

~Proverb

Imitation is the sincerest form of flattery.

~Proverb

∽

Happiness lies in the joy of achievement and the thrill of creative effort.

~Franklin D. Roosevelt

∽

Do what you can, with what you have, where you are.

~Theodore Roosevelt

∽

Of course there is no formula for success except perhaps an unconditional acceptance of life and what it brings.

~Arthur Rubinstein

∽

I cannot give you the formula for success, but I can give you the formula for failure—which is: Try to please everybody.

~Herbert Bayard Swope

∾

Plain question and plain answer make the shortest road out of most perplexities.

~Mark Twain

∾

Some people dream of success while others wake up and work hard at it.

~Author Unknown

∾

Success is blocked by concentrating on it and planning for it... Success is shy—it won't come out while you're watching.

~Tennessee Williams

∾

Success is simply a matter of luck. Ask any failure.

~Earl Wilson

∾

Never mistake activity for achievement.

~ John Wooden

Simplicity

It is simplicity that makes the uneducated more effective than
the educated when addressing popular audiences.

~Aristotle

It is the greatest adornment of art.

As I grew older, I realized that it was much better to insist on
the genuine forms of nature, for simplicity is
the greatest adornment of art.

~Albrecht Dürer

Most of the fundamental ideas of science are essentially
simple, and may, as a rule, be expressed in
a language comprehensible to everyone.

~Albert Einstein

Nothing is more simple than greatness; indeed,
to be simple is to be great.
~*Ralph Waldo Emerson*

∽

Let us learn to live simply, so that others may simply live.
~*Mahatma Gandhi*

∽

The obvious is that which is never seen until someone expresses
it simply.
~*Kahlil Gibran*

∽

Nothing is true, but that which is simple.
~*Johann Wolfgang von Goethe*

∽

Simplicity of character is the natural result of profound thought.
~*William Hazlitt*

∽

I would not give a fig for the simplicity this side of complexity,
but I would give my life for the simplicity on the other side of
complexity.
~*Oliver Wendell Holmes, Sr.*

∽

Fishing is much more than fish. It is the great occasion when we may return to the fine simplicity of our forefathers.

~Herbert Hoover

᠙

The sculptor produces the beautiful statue by chipping away such parts of the marble block as are not needed—it is a process of elimination.

~Elbert Hubbard

᠙

That's been one of my mantras—focus and simplicity. Simple can be harder than complex: You have to work hard to get your thinking clean to make it simple. But it's worth it in the end because once you get there, you can move mountains.

~Steve Jobs

᠙

I have learned by some experience, by many examples, and by the writings of countless others before me, also occupied in the search, that certain environments, certain modes of life, certain rules of conduct are more conducive to inner and outer harmony than others. There are, in fact, certain roads that one may follow. Simplification of life is one of them.

~Anne Morrow Lindbergh

᠙

Simplicity and naturalness are the truest marks of distinction.

~W. Somerset Maugham

∾

I take a simple view of living. It is,
keep your eyes open and get on with it.

~Sir Laurence Olivier

∾

We struggle with the complexities and avoid the simplicities.

~Norman Vincent Peale

∾

Beauty of style and harmony and grace and
good rhythm depend on simplicity.

~Plato

∾

Of manners gentle, of affections mild;
In wit, a man; simplicity, a child.

~Alexander Pope

There is a certain majesty in simplicity which
is far above all the quaintness of wit.

~Alexander Pope

∾

From native simplicity we arrive at more profound simplicity.

~Albert Schweitzer

∾

Most of the luxuries, and many of the so-called comforts
of life, are not only not indispensable, but positive
hindrances to the elevation of mankind. With respect to
luxuries and comforts, the wisest have ever lived
a more simple and meagre life than the poor.

~Henry David Thoreau

To be a philosopher is not merely to have subtle thoughts,
nor even to found a school, but so to love wisdom as
to live according to its dictates, a life
of simplicity, independence, magnanimity and trust.

~Henry David Thoreau

Simplicity, simplicity, simplicity! I say, let your
affairs be as two or three, and not a hundred or a
thousand; instead of a million count half a dozen,
and keep your accounts on your thumb nail.

~Henry David Thoreau

∾

There is no greatness where there is
not simplicity, goodness, and truth.

~Leo Tolstoy

∾

Manifest plainness, embrace simplicity,
reduce selfishness, have few desires.

~Lao Tzu

Simplicity is the glory of expression.

~Walt Whitman

The truth is rarely pure, and never simple.

~Oscar Wilde

Organic architecture seeks superior sense of use and a finer
sense of comfort, expressed in organic simplicity.

~Frank Lloyd Wright

Simplicity and repose are the qualities that
measure the true value of any work of art.

~Frank Lloyd Wright

"Think simple" as my old master used to say—meaning reduce
the whole of its parts into the simplest terms, getting back to
first principles.

~Frank Lloyd Wright

Win or Lose

If you wish success in life, make perseverance your bosom friend, experience your wise counselor, caution your elder brother and hope your guardian genius.

~Joseph Addison

To become an able and successful man in any profession, three things are necessary, nature, study and practice.

~Henry Ward Beecher

Before anything else, preparation is the key to success.

~Alexander Graham Bell

The art of losing isn't hard to master;
so many things seem filled with the intent
to be lost that their loss is no disaster.

~Elizabeth Bishop

Nothing in the world can take the place of Persistence. Talent will not; nothing is more common than unsuccessful men with talent. Genius will not; unrewarded genius is almost a proverb. Education will not; the world is full of educated derelicts. Persistence and determination alone are omnipotent. The slogan "Press On" has solved and always will solve the problems of the human race.

~Calvin Coolidge

The person who makes a success of living is the one who sees his goal steadily and aims for it unswervingly. That is dedication.

~Cecil B. DeMille

Success is counted sweetest
By those who ne'er succeed.

~Emily Dickinson

Many of life's failures are people who did not realize how close they were to success when they gave up.

~Thomas A. Edison

It is only as we develop others that we permanently succeed.

~Harvey S. Firestone

Only connect!

~*E. M. Forster*

෧෨

Do good to your friends to keep them,
to your enemies to win them.

~*Benjamin Franklin*

෧෨

Don't be discouraged by a failure. It can be a positive experience. Failure is, in a sense, the highway to success, inasmuch as
every discovery of what is false leads us to seek earnestly after
what is true, and every fresh experience points out some form of
error which we shall afterwards carefully avoid.

~*John Keats*

෧෨

We didn't lose the game; we just ran out of time.

~*Vince Lombardi*

Winners never quit and quitters never win.

~*Vince Lombardi*

Winning is not a sometime thing; it's an all time thing. You
don't win once in a while, you don't do things right once in a
while, you do them right all the time. Winning is habit.
Unfortunately, so is losing.

~*Vince Lombardi*

෧෨

Better late than never.

~*Titus Livius*

❧

There is nothing more difficult to take in hand, more perilous to conduct, or more certain in its success, than to take the lead in the introduction of a new order of things.

~*Niccolò Machiavelli*

❧

By losing your goal, you have lost your way.

~*Friedrich Nietzsche*

❧

Don't look back. Something might be gaining on you.

~*Satchel Paige*

❧

The more you lose yourself in something bigger than yourself, the more energy you will have.

~*Norman Vincent Peale*

❧

It's not whether you win or lose, it's how you play the game.

~*Grantland Rice*

❧

Our doubts are traitors, and make us lose the good we oft
might win, by fearing to attempt.

~William Shakespeare

∾

You may be disappointed if you fail,
but you are doomed if you don't try.

~Beverly Sills

∾

Ring out the old, ring in the new,
Ring, happy bells, across the snow:
The year is going, let him go;
Ring out the false, ring in the true.

~Alfred Lord Tennyson

∾

Success usually comes to those who are
too busy to be looking for it.

~Henry David Thoreau

∾

By letting it go it all gets done. The world is won by
those who let it go. But when you try and try.
The world is beyond the winning.

~Lao Tzu

∾

Make service your first priority,
not success and success will follow.

~Author Unknown

Successful leaders have the courage to
take action where others hesitate.

~Author Unknown

One should always play fairly when one has the winning cards.

~Oscar Wilde

Material possessions, winning scores, and great reputations are
meaningless in the eyes of the Lord, because He knows what we
really are and that is all that matters.

~John Wooden

Winning takes talent, to repeat takes character.

~John Wooden

Appendices

Appendix: Favorite Quotes

Quote:_____

_____

_____

Quote:_____

_____

_____

Quote:_____

_____

_____

Quote:_____

_____

_____

Quote:_____

_____

_____

Appendix: Success Checklist

Accomplishments

Successes …

_____

_____

_____

_____

_____

_____

_____

_____

_____

_____

_____

_____

_____

_____

_____

_____

_____

_____

_____

_____

Attributes

Successes …

_____

_____

_____

_____

_____

_____

_____

_____

_____

_____

_____

Goals

Successes …

_____

_____

_____

_____

_____

_____

_____

_____

_____

_____

_____

Family

Successes …

_____
_____
_____
_____
_____
_____
_____
_____
_____
_____
_____
_____

Friendships

Successes …

_____
_____
_____
_____
_____
_____
_____
_____
_____
_____
_____
_____

Life

Successes ...

_____

_____

_____

_____

_____

_____

_____

_____

_____

_____

_____

_____

Little Things

Successes ...

_____

_____

_____

_____

_____

_____

_____

_____

_____

_____

_____

_____

Money

Successes ...

_____

_____

_____

_____

_____

_____

_____

_____

_____

_____

_____

_____

Things I Never Expected

Successes ...

_____

_____

_____

_____

_____

_____

_____

_____

_____

_____

_____

_____

Work

Successes ...

_____

_____

_____

_____

_____

_____

_____

_____

_____

_____

_____

_____

Other

Successes ...

_____

_____

_____

_____

_____

_____

_____

_____

_____

_____

_____

_____

Appendix: Success Journal

January:_____

_____

_____

_____

_____

_____

_____

_____

_____

_____

February:_____

_____

_____

_____

_____

_____

_____

_____

_____

_____

March:_____

_____

_____

_____

_____

_____

_____

_____

_____

April:_____

_____

_____

_____

_____

_____

_____

_____

_____

May:_____

_____

_____

_____

_____

_____

_____

_____

_____

June:_____

_____

_____

_____

_____

_____

_____

_____

_____

July:_____

_____

_____

_____

_____

_____

_____

_____

_____

August:_____

_____

_____

_____

_____

_____

_____

_____

_____

September:_____

_____

_____

_____

_____

_____

_____

_____

_____

October:_____

_____

_____

_____

_____

_____

_____

_____

_____

November:_____

_____

_____

_____

_____

_____

_____

_____

_____

December:_____

_____

_____

_____

_____

_____

_____

_____

_____

_____

_____

Biographical Index

Biographical Index

Addison, Joseph: 1672-1719, English essayist and poet
Amiel, Henri-Frédéric: 1821-1881, Swiss philosopher and poet
Anthony, Susan B.: 1820-1906, American civil rights leader
Aretino, Pietro: 1492-1556, Italian author and poet
Aristotle: 384-322 BC, Greek philosopher
Ashe, Arthur: 1943-1993, American professional tennis player
Aurelius, Marcus: 121-180, Roman Emperor

Bacon, Francis: 1566-1626, English philosopher
Ball, Lucille: 1911-1989, American comedian
Bashō, Matsuo: 1644-1694, Japanese poet
Beecher, Henry Ward: 1813-1887, American clergyman
Bell, Alexander Graham: 1847-1922, American inventor
Berlin, Irving: 1888-1989, American composer
Bernstein, Leonard: 1918-1990, American conductor
Billings, Josh: 1818-1885, American writer
Bishop, Elizabeth: 1911-1979, American poet
Bottome, Phillis: 1884-1963, British novelist
Brande, Dorothea: 1893-1948, American editor and writer
Browning, Elizabeth Barrett: 1806-1861, English poet
Bryan, William Jennings: 1860-1925, American politician
Buck, Pearl S.: 1892-1973, American writer
Buddha: 563-483 BC, Spiritual teacher

Burnham, David: 1846-1912, American architect and urban planner

Buscaglia, Felice Leonardo "Leo": 1924-1998: American author and lecturer

Camus, Albert: 1913-1960, French writer

Carnegie, Andrew: 1835-1919, Scottish-American entrepreneur

Carnegie, Dale: 1888-1955, American lecturer and writer

Carroll, Lewis: 1832-1898, English author

Carson, Johnny: 1925-2005, American comedian

Carver, George Washington: 1864-1943, American inventor and scientist

Casals, Pablo: 1876-1973, Spanish cellist

Casteneda, Carlos: 1925-1998, Peruvian-American anthropoligist and author

Chaplin, Charlie: 1889-1977, English comedic actor

Churchill, Winston: 1875-1965, British politician

Confucius: 551-479 BC, Chinese philosopher

Coolidge, Calvin: 1872-1933, American President of the United States

Cronkite, Walter: 1916-2009, American broadcast journalist

Darwin, Charles: 1809-1882, English scientist

Dean, James: 1931-1955, American film actor

Deming, W. Edwards: 1900-1993, American author and consultant

DeMille, Cecile B.: 1881-1959, American film director and producer

Descartes, René: 1596-1650, French philosopher and writer

de Unamuno, Miguel: 1864-1936, Spanish essayist and poet

Dickinson, Emily: 1830-1886, American poet

Disraeli, Benjamin: 1804-1881, British Prime Minister

Drucker, Peter: 1909-2005, American writer and management consultant

Dürer, Albrecht: 1471-1528, German painter and printer

Earhart, Amelia: 1897-1937, American aviation pioneer and author
Edison, Thomas: 1847-1931, American inventor
Einstein, Albert: 1879-1955, German-Swiss philosopher
Eliot, George: 1819-1880, English novelist
Eliot, T.S.: 1888-1965, American poet
Ellis, Albert: 1913-2007, American psychologist
Emerson, Ralph Waldo: 1803-1882, American writer and poet
Epictetus: 55-135, Greek philosopher

Feather, William: 1889-1981, American author and publisher
Firestone, Harvey S.: 1868-1938, American businessman and entrepreneur
Ford, Henry: 1863-1947, American businessman and entrepreneur
Forster, E.M.: 1879-1970, English novelist
Fosse, Bob: 1927-1987, American actor, dancer, and theater choreographer
Fowler, Gene: 1890-1960, American journalist
Franklin, Benjamin: 1706-1790, American author and statesman
Friedan, Betty: 1921-2006, American author
Frost, Robert: 1874-1963, American poet

Gandhi, Mahatma: 1869-1948, Indian political leader
Getty, J. Paul: 1892-1976, American industrialist
Gibran, Kahlil: 1883-1931, Lebanese-American writer and poet
von Goethe, Johann Wolfgang: 1749-1832, German writer
Gracián, Baltasar: 1601-1658, Spanish writer
Grant, Cary: 1904-1986, English-American actor

Hamilton, Alexander: 1755-1804, American Founding Father
Hazlitt, William: 1778-1830, American businessman
Heller, Joseph: 1921-1999, American writer
Hemingway, Ernest: 1899-1961, American writer
Hendrix, Jimi: 1942-1970, American singer and song writer

Hepburn, Audrey: 1929-1993, British actress
Herbert, George: 1593-1633, Welsh poet
Hill, Napoleon: 1883-1970, American writer
Holmes, Sr., Oliver Wendell: 1809-1894, American author and physician
Hoover, Herbert: 1874-1964, American President of the United States
Hope, Bob: 1903-2003, British-American comedian
Hubbard, Elbert: 1856-1915, American writer
Hugo, Victor: 1802-1885, French poet and writer

Irving, Washington: 1783-1859, American author and historian

James, William: 1842-1910, American psychologist
Jobs, Steve: 1955-2011, American businessman and entrepreneur
Johnson, Lyndon B.: 1908-1973, American President of the United States
Johnson, Samuel: 1709-1784, English author
Jung, Carl: 1875-1961, Swiss psychiatrist

Kant, Immanuel: 1724-1804, German philosopher
Karr, Alphonse: 1808-1890, French novelist
Keats, John: 1795-1821, English poet
Keller, Helen: 1880-1968, American writer
Kennedy, Jackie: 1929-1994, First Lady of the United States and editor
Kennedy, John Fitzgerald: 1917-1963, American President of the United States
Keynes, John Maynard: 1883-1946, British economist
Kierkegaard, Søren: 1813-1855, Danish philosopher
King, Jr., Martin Luther: 1929-1968, American clergyman
Kipling, Rudyard: 1865-1936, English writer
Kroc, Ray: 1902-1984, American businessman and entrepreneur

la Rochefoucald, François, Duc de: 1613-1680, French writer
Leacock, Stephen: 1869-1944, English-Canadian writer
Lincoln, Abraham: 1809-1865, American President of the United States
Lindbergh, Anne Morrow: 1906-2001, American aviator and writer
Livius, Titus: 59 BC-17 AD, Roman historian and author
Lombardi, Vince: 1913-1970, Italian-American football coach
Longfellow, Henry Wadsworth: 1807-1882, American poet
Luckman, Charles: 1909-1999, American architect

Macchiavelli, Niccolò: 1469-1527, Italian historian and writer
Mandino, Og: 1923-1996, American author
Maslow, Abraham: 1908-1970, American professor of psychology
Massieu, Jean: 1772-1849, French educator
Maugham, W. Somerset: 1874-1965, English playwright
Mead, Margaret: 1901-1978, American anthropologist
Merton, Thomas: 1915-1968, American writer
Monroe, Marilyn: 1926-1962, American actress
Morley, Christopher: 1890-1957, American journalist and poet
Mumford, Lewis: 1895-1990, American historian, literary critic, and writer

Nightingale, Earl: 1921-1989, American author and motivational speaker
Nietzsche, Friedrich: 1844-1900, German philosopher

Olivier, Sir Lawrence: 1907-1989, English actor and director
Orwell, George: 1903-1950, English author

Paige, Satchel: 1906-1982, American baseball player
Pareto, Vilfredo: 1848-1923, Italian economist
Parks, Rosa: 1913-2005, American civil rights activist
Patton, George Smith: 1885-1945, American general

Pavese, Cesare: 1908-1950, Italian poet
Pavlova, Anna: 1881-1931, Russian ballerina
Peale, Norman Vincent: 1898-1993, American author
Pacasso, Pablo: 1881-1973, Spanish painter
Plato: 428-348 BC, Greek philosopher
Pope, Alexander: 1688-1744, English poet
Presley, Elvis: 1935-1977, American singer and song writer
Princess Diana: 1961-1997, English celebrity and philanthropist
Proust, Marcel: 1871-1922, French novelist
Pryor, Richard: 1940-2002, American comedian

Rand, Ayn: 1905-1982, Russian-American novelist
Rice, Grantland: 1880-1954, American sportswriter
Rockefeller, Jr, John D.: 1874-1960, American philanthropist
Rogers, Will: 1879-1935, American comedian
Roosevelt, Eleanor: 1884-1962, First Lady of the United States and writer
Roosevelt, Franklin D.: 1882-1945, American President of the United States
Roosevelt, Theodore: 1858-1919, American President of the United States
Rossetti, Christina: 1830-1894, English poet
Rubenstein, Arthur: 1887-1982, Polish-American pianist
Rumi: 1207-1273, Persian poet
Ruskin, John: 1819-1900, English author and poet

Sandburg, Carl: 1878-1967, American poet and writer
Schopenhauer, Arthur: 1788-1860, German philosopher
Schweitzer, Albert: 1875-1965, Franco-German theologian
Seneca: 4 BC–65 AD, Roman philosopher
Dr. Seuss (Theodor Seuss Giesel): 1904-1991, American writer
Shakespeare, William: 1564-1616, English poet and playwright
Shore, Dinah: 1916-1994, American actress and television personality

Sills, Beverly: 1929-2002, American operatic soprano
Socrates: 469-399 BC, Greek philosopher
Steinbeck, John: 1902-1968, American writer
Stevenson, Robert Louis: 1850-1894, Scottish novelist and poet
Stone, W. Clement: 1902-2002, American author and businessman
Swift, Jonathan: 1667-1745, Anglo-Irish poet and writer
Swope, Herbert Bayard: 1882-1958, American editor and journalist

Taylor, Elizabeth: 1932-2011, British-American actress
Teasdale, Sara: 1884-1933, American poet
Tennyson, Alfred Lord: 1809-1892, English poet and writer
Teresa, Mother: 1910-1997, Albanian nun
Terence: 185-159 BC, Roman playwright
Thayer, Ernest L.: 1863-1940, American poet
Thoreau, Henry David: 1817-1862, American writer and poet
Tolstoy, Leo: 1828-1910, Russian writer
Truman, Harry S.: 1884-1972, American President of the
United States
Twain, Mark: 1835-1910, American writer
Tzu, Lao: 350-250 BC, Chinese philosopher

van Gogh, Vincent: 1853-1890, Dutch painter
da Vinci, Leonardo: 1452-1519, Italian painter and writer
Virgil: 70-19 BC, Roman poet

Walpole, Robert: 1676-1745, British statesman
Ward, William Arthur: 1921-1994, American writer
Warner, Charles, Dudley: 1829-1900, American novelist
Washington, Booker T.: 1856-1915, American author and educator
Washington, George: 1732-1799, American President of the
United States
Wattles, Wallace D.: 1860-1911, American writer
White, E.B.: 1899-1985, American writer
Whitman, Walt: 1819-1892, American poet

Wilde, Oscar: 1854-1900, Irish writer
Williams, Tennessee: 1911-1983, American writer
Wilson, Earl: 1907-1987, American journalist
Wooden, John: 1910-2010, American basketball coach
Wordsworth, William: 1770-1850, English poet
Wright, Frank Lloyd: 1867-1959, American architect
Wu Men: 1183-1260, Chinese poet

Yeats, William Butler: 1865-1939, Irish poet

Index

Index

Addison, Joseph: 91
Amiel, Henri-Frédéric: 59
Anthony, Susan B.: 11
Aretino, Pietro: 67
Aristotle: 3, 83
Ashe, Arthur: 27
Aurelius, Marcus: 43

Bacon, Francis: 35, 59, 67
Ball, Lucille: 51
Bashō, Matsuo: 27
Beecher, Henry Ward: 75, 91
Bell, Alexander Graham: 91
Berlin, Irving: 75
Bernstein, Leonard: 3
Bible: 19, 59, 60
Billings, Josh: 43
Bishop, Elizabeth: 91
Bottome, Phillis: 67
Brande, Dorothea: 67
Browning, Elizabeth Barrett: 27
Bryan, William Jennings: 51
Buck, Pearl S.: 75
Buddha: 11, 19, 27, 68

Burnham, David: 3
Buscaglia, Leo: 51

Camus, Albert: 60
Carnegie, Andrew: 4, 51, 52
Carnegie, Dale: 75, 76
Carroll, Lewis: 28
Carson, Johnny: 19
Carver, George Washington: 60
Casals, Pablo: 60
Casteneda, Carlos: 11
Chaplin, Charlie: 43
Churchill, Winston: 28, 44, 68, 76
Confucius: 11, 35, 44, 52
Coolidge, Calvin: 92
Cronkite, Walter: 76

Darwin, Charles: 44
Dean, James: 4
Deming, W. Edwards: 35
DeMille, Cecile B.: 92
Descartes, René: 36
de Unamuno, Miguel: 36
Dickinson, Emily: 36, 52, 76, 92

Disraeli, Benjamin: 36
Drucker, Peter: 19
Dürer, Albrecht: 83

Earhart, Amelia: 4
Edison, Thomas: 92
Einstein, Albert: 4, 28, 36, 37, 68, 76, 83
Eliot, George: 52
Eliot, T.S.: 37
Ellis, Albert: 12, 44
Emerson, Ralph Waldo: 4, 12, 28, 44, 84
Epictetus: 52, 69

Feather, William: 77
Firestone, Harvey S.: 92
Ford, Henry: 4, 20, 53
Forster, E.M.: 45, 93
Fosse, Bob: 60
Fowler, Gene: 77
Franklin, Benjamin: 20, 29, 37, 93
Friedan, Betty: 20
Frost, Robert: 45

Gandhi, Mahatma: 69, 84
Getty, J. Paul: 21
Gibran, Kahlil: 61, 84
von Goethe, Johann Wolfgang: 29, 77, 84
Gracián, Balthasar: 53
Grant, Cary: 45

Hamilton, Alexander: 69
Haszlitt, William: 84
Heller, Joseph: 69
Hemingway, Ernest: 12
Hendrix, Jimi: 53

Hepburn, Audrey: 37, 61, 69
Herbert, George: 45
Hill, Napoleon: 5, 12, 53, 70
Holmes, Sr. Oliver Wendell: 5, 13, 37, 84
Hoover, Herbert: 85
Hope, Bob: 61
Hubbard, Elbert: 5, 53, 77, 85
Hugo, Victor: 5

Irving, Washington: 70

James, William: 45
Jobs, Steve: 5, 13, 21, 77, 85
Johnson, Lyndon B.: 29, 54
Johnson, Samuel: 54
Jung, Carl: 46

Kant, Immanuel: 46
Karr, Alphonse: 21
Keats, John: 93
Keller, Helen: 46, 70, 78
Kennedy, Jackie: 54
Kennedy, John Fitzgerald: 6, 37, 70
Keynes, John Maynard: 6
Kierkegaard, Søren: 46
King, Jr., Martin Luther: 6
Kipling, Rudyard: 78
Kroc, Ray: 21, 78

la Rochefoucauld, François, Duc de: 21
Leacock, Stephen: 29
Lincoln, Abraham: 6, 29, 38, 61, 78
Lindbergh, Anne Morrow: 85
Livius, Titus: 94

Lombardi, Vince: 38, 93
Longfellow, Henry Wadsworth: 13, 22, 46
Luckman, Charles: 38

Macchiavelli, Niccolò: 71, 94
Mandino, Og: 29, 30
Maslow, Abraham: 13
Massieu, Jean: 13
Maugham, W. Somerset: 86
Mead, Margaret: 38
Merton, Thomas: 54
Monroe, Marilyn: 54
Morley, Christopher: 14
Mumford, Lewis: 47

Nightingale, Earl: 14
Nietzsche, Friedrich: 94

Olivier, Sir Lawrence: 86
Orwell, George: 6

Paige, Satchel: 94
Pareto, Vilfredo: 38
Parks, Rosa: 71
Patton, George Smith: 78
Pavese, Cesare: 30
Pavlova, Anna: 79
Peale, Norman Vincent: 7, 14, 86, 94
Picasso, Pablo: 7, 61
Plato: 47, 86
Pope, Alexander: 14, 86
Presley, Elvis: 54
Princess Diana: 30, 39
Proust, Marcel: 55
Proverbs: 7, 22, 30, 39, 55, 62, 71, 79
Pryor, Richard: 62

Rand, Ayn: 31
Rice, Grantland: 94
Rockefeller, Jr., John D.: 22
Rogers, Will: 22, 39
Roosevelt, Eleanor: 14, 31, 39, 55, 62
Roosevelt, Franklin D.: 79
Roosevelt, Theodore: 79
Rossetti, Christina, 31
Rubinstein, Arthur: 79
Rumi: 15
Ruskin, John: 22

Sandburg, Carl: 31, 47
Schopenhauer, Arthur: 55
Schweitzer, Albert: 87
Seneca: 23
Dr. Seuss: 15
Shakespeare, William: 15, 47, 62, 95
Shore, Dinah: 62
Sills, Beverly: 95
Socrates: 23, 31
Steinbeck, John: 56
Stevenson, Robert Louis: 15, 32, 47
Stone, W. Clement: 7, 56
Swift, Jonathan: 48
Swope, Herbert Bayard: 80

Talmud: 23
Taylor, Elizabeth: 63
Teasdale, Sara: 48
Tennyson, Alfred Lord: 7, 56, 95
Teresa, Mother: 63
Terence: 71
Thayer, Ernest L.: 63
Thoreau, Henry David: 7, 48, 87, 95
Tolstoy, Leo: 32, 87

Truman, Harry S.: 56
Twain, Mark: 23, 39, 63, 80
Tzu, Lao: 8, 23, 40, 88, 95

Author Unknown: 8, 15, 16, 24,
    32, 48, 63, 64, 71, 80, 96

van Gogh, Vincent: 40
da Vinci, Leonardo: 16, 72
Virgil: 8

Walpole, Robert: 40
Ward, William Arthur: 64
Warner, Charles Dudley: 24, 32

Washington, Booker T.: 72
Washington, George: 56
Wattles, Wallace D.: 8
White, E.B.: 64
Whitman, Walt: 16, 24, 88
Wilde, Oscar: 16, 24, 40, 88, 96
Williams, Tennessee: 80
Wilson, Earl: 80
Wooden, John: 80, 96
Wordsworth, William: 24
Wright, Frank Lloyd: 88
Wu Men: 48

Yeats, William Butler: 8

Kathleen Welton specializes in print and online publishing project initiatives. She collaborates with authors and organizations in the areas of business and strategic planning; content and new product development; marketing, sales, and distribution. During her career, she has had the opportunity to develop award-winning books, series, and Web sites while working with the American Bar Association, Dearborn Trade, Dow Jones-Irwin, H&R Block, IDG Books, National Book Network, and John Wiley & Sons. Her published books include: *The Little Book of Gratitude Quotes*, *The Little Book of Success Quotes*, *The Little Journal of Gratitude*, *100 Essential Modern Poems by Women* (co-edited with Joseph Parisi), and *Poetry For Beginners* (co-authored with Margaret Chapman). She earned a BA degree in English and Italian Literature from Stanford University.

CPSIA information can be obtained at www.ICGtesting.com
Printed in the USA
LVOW112128210312

274239LV00007B/10/P

9 780615 516813